CONTENTS

USING THIS GUIDE   **1**

Considerations for Teaching Graphic Novels   2

Indigenous Perspectives and History   2

Considerations for Teaching the Surviving the City Series   4

Inviting an Elder Into Your Learning Space   4

CURRICULUM CONNECTIONS   **6**

British Columbia: English First Peoples Literary Studies 10   6

British Columbia: English First Peoples: Literary Studies + Spoken Language 11   8

British Columbia: English First Peoples 12   11

Manitoba: Senior 1 English Language Arts   14

Manitoba: Senior 2 English Language Arts   16

Manitoba: Senior 3 English Language Arts   18

Manitoba: Senior 4 English Language Arts   20

Manitoba: Grade 12 Global Issues: Citizenship and Sustainability   22

Manitoba: Grade 12 Current Topics in First Nations, Métis, and Inuit Studies   23

Ontario: Grade 9 English Language Arts (Academic)   24

Ontario: Grade 10 English Language Arts (Academic)   26

Ontario: Grade 11 English Language Arts (University Prep)   26

Ontario: Grade 11 English Language Arts (Reading and Literature Studies)   27

Ontario: Grade 12 English Language Arts (University Prep)   28

Ontario: Grade 12 English Language Arts (Reading and Literature Studies)   28

Ontario: Grade 11 and 12 First Nations, Métis, and Inuit Studies   29

LESSON 1: How Do We Read Graphic Novels?   32

LESSON 2: Why Is Culture Important?   38

LESSON 3: What Is Wellness From an Indigenous Perspective?   43

LESSON 4: How Can I Make a Difference?   49

- Indspire https://indspire.ca/for-educators/
- National Centre for Truth and Reconciliation https://education.nctr.ca/link-to-page-2/
  Note that new versions of this teacher guide will be released along with new titles in the Surviving the City series.

CONSIDERATIONS FOR TEACHING GRAPHIC NOVELS

The terms *graphic novel* and *comics* describe the format of a book, rather than a genre. Graphic novels and comic books can be fiction, nonfiction, biography, fantasy, dystopia, or any genre in between.[1] Graphic novels are an accessible reading resource for all students, and they have been proven to engage even the most reluctant of readers.[2] Graphic novels also include dialogue, characters' thoughts, narration, and captions. Graphic novels are meant to be read from left to right, and top to bottom.

The first lesson in this guide is designed to introduce teachers and students alike to this format. For more information and ideas for using graphic novels in the classroom, see the resource *Teaching With Graphic Novels* by Shelley Stagg Peterson, available through Portage & Main Press.

INDIGENOUS PERSPECTIVES AND HISTORY

Indigenous perspectives are now part of the curriculum in every province in Canada. Further, the National Truth and Reconciliation Commission's Calls to Action #62 and #63 deal directly with Indigenous education, stating:

62. We call upon the federal, provincial, and territorial governments, in consultation and collaboration with Survivors, Aboriginal peoples, and educators, to:

    i. Make age-appropriate curriculum on residential schools, Treaties, and Aboriginal peoples' historical and contemporary contributions to Canada a mandatory education requirement for Kindergarten to Grade Twelve students.
    ii. Provide the necessary funding to post-secondary institutions to educate teachers on how to integrate Indigenous knowledge and teaching methods into classrooms.
    iii. Provide the necessary funding to Aboriginal schools to utilize Indigenous knowledge and teaching methods in classrooms.
    iv. Establish senior-level positions in government at the assistant deputy minister level or higher dedicated to Aboriginal content in education.

63. We call upon the Council of Ministers of Education, Canada to maintain an annual commitment to Aboriginal education issues, including:

1 "What is a Graphic Novel?" Get Graphic, the Buffalo and Erie County Public Library and Partnering Organizations, accessed August 1, 2019, https://www.buffalolib.org/content/get-graphic/what-graphic-novel.

2 Knutson, Sarah. "How Graphic Novels Help Students Develop Critical Skills," Room 241: A Blog by Concordia University-Portland, updated October 23, 2018, https://education.cu-portland.edu/blog/classroom-resources/graphic-novels-visual-literacy/.

i. Developing and implementing Kindergarten to Grade Twelve curriculum and learning resources on Aboriginal peoples in Canadian history, and the history and legacy of residential schools.

ii. Sharing information and best practices on teaching curriculum related to residential schools and Aboriginal history.

iii. Building student capacity for intercultural understanding, empathy, and mutual respect.

iv. Identifying teacher-training needs relating to the above.[3]

Aspects of Indigenous pedagogy are woven throughout this teacher guide to enhance students' understanding of Indigenous worldviews. Circle pedagogy is used throughout this resource as a way to show the interconnectedness of ideas and topics, namely in the form of the medicine wheel as a graphic organizer. The medicine wheel is an ancient symbol representing interconnectedness, balance, and holism that has been adapted for modern audiences as a graphic organizer to visually represent relationships between concepts in groups of four. Students will have the opportunity to select, research, and present on an Indigenous resistance movement.

According to the Manitoba Education and Youth's *Integrating Aboriginal Perspectives into Curricula* document (2003), implementing Indigenous perspectives has a number of positive effects in the classroom including:

- helping Indigenous students develop a positive self-identity through learning their own histories, cultures, traditional values, contemporary lifestyles, and traditional knowledge
- helping Indigenous students to participate in a learning environment that will equip them with the knowledge and skills needed to participate more fully in the unique civic and cultural realities of their communities
- helping non-Indigenous students develop an understanding and respect for the histories, traditional values, contemporary lifestyles, and traditional knowledge of Indigenous Peoples
- helping non-Indigenous students develop informed opinions on matters relating to Indigenous Peoples[4]

---

3   Truth and Reconciliation Commission of Canada. *Truth and Reconciliation Commission of Canada: Calls to Action* (2015), 7.

4   Manitoba Education and Youth. *Integrating Aboriginal Perspectives into Curricula: A Resource for Curriculum Developers, Teachers, and Administrators.* 2003.

SURVIVING THE CITY TEACHER GUIDE © 2019 PORTAGE & MAIN PRESS ISBN: 978-1-55379-904-7

CONSIDERATIONS FOR TEACHING THE SURVIVING THE CITY SERIES

Sensitive themes are likely to come up when reading the Surviving the City series and learning about Indigenous topics. This graphic novel deals with sensitive topics such as racism, caregiver illness, the child welfare system, residential schools, and Missing and Murdered Indigenous Women and Girls and Two-Spirit People. It is important that you inform your students about resources that are available to them if they should feel overwhelmed or triggered at any point throughout readings. Teachers should also create a safe and open learning environment where students' mental health is supported. Often, having direct discussions about mental health and wellness is a great way for students to hear from others and learn positive coping skills to help them through their learning journeys. Lesson 3: What Is Wellness From an Indigenous Perspective? touches on the subject of wellness through an Indigenous lens and guides students through a medicine-wheel wellness activity.

INVITING AN ELDER INTO YOUR LEARNING SPACE

Teachers may want to engage the larger community and invite an Elder or Knowledge Keeper into their classroom to share stories, knowledge, or teachings with the class. Here are some guidelines on building a positive relationship with a local Elder or Knowledge Keeper. Manitoba Education and Youth defines an Elder as "any person regarded or chosen by an Aboriginal nation to be the keeper and teacher of its oral tradition and knowledge," but it is important to remember that this definition may vary from community to community.[5]

PREPARING TO MEET WITH AN ELDER

- Ask your local school board if they have an Elder-in-residence or a trusted Elder or Knowledge Keeper that they often ask to speak with students. You should always try to invite a local Elder first.
- Research the local protocols for inviting an Elder to speak with your class. Often, this will involve the passing of tobacco.
- Arrange a meeting between you and the Elder well in advance of the visit to your class.

MEETING WITH AN ELDER

- Share a bit about yourself and your family's history.
- Listen and learn from the Elder.
- Adhere to the protocols in your area, and ask the Elder if they would be interested in sharing their gifts with your class.
- Be as flexible about the day and time for the visit as you can. Decide this together!

---

5   Manitoba Education and Youth. *Integrating Aboriginal Perspectives into Curricula: A Resource for Curriculum Developers, Teachers, and Administrators.* 2003.

SURVIVING THE CITY TEACHER GUIDE © 2019 PORTAGE & MAIN PRESS   ISBN: 978-1-55379-904-7

- Ask if the Elder needs any special accommodations for when they come.
- Discuss fair compensation. The Elder may be taking the day off from work to accommodate your needs, so it is essential that they are well compensated for their time, energy, and emotional labour.
- Ask the Elder how they would like to be introduced to your class, and respect their preferences.

PREPARING YOUR STUDENTS FOR AN ELDER'S VISIT
- Inform students that an Elder will be visiting the class. Ask if anyone knows what an Elder is, and discuss the important roles they have in our communities. Share that Elders are people who hold sacred teachings and should be treated with the utmost respect.
- Share with students why you decided to bring an Elder into the classroom.
- Ask if any students would like to volunteer to give the Elder a tobacco tie (depending on the protocol of your region). Brief students about the protocol, and why it is important to thank the Elder in this way.

DAY OF THE VISIT TO YOUR CLASS
- Welcome the Elder to your class/school. Have a student present the Elder with the tobacco tie (depending on the protocol in your region).
- Give the Elder a tour of your school, if possible, or at least make sure they know where the washrooms are.
- Ensure that students are respectful while the Elder is speaking.
- Thank the Elder at the end and present them with the honorarium.

Try to build a relationship with a local Elder or Knowledge Keeper. Relationships take time to develop, so you should contact the Elder as soon as possible. If the day goes well, make sure to let them know that you will be inviting them back again. You could also have students write a thank-you card to the Elder as a way of showing appreciation.

SURVIVING THE CITY TEACHER GUIDE © 2019 PORTAGE & MAIN PRESS ISBN: 978-1-55379-904-7

CURRICULUM CONNECTIONS

BRITISH COLUMBIA: ENGLISH FIRST PEOPLES LITERARY STUDIES 10

SURVIVING THE CITY TEACHER GUIDE © 2019 PORTAGE & MAIN PRESS ISBN: 978-1-55379-904-7

Curricular Competencies [6] Using oral, written, visual, and digital texts, students are expected individually and collaboratively to be able to:	Lesson			
	1	2	3	4
Recognize and appreciate the role of story, narrative, and oral tradition in expressing First Peoples perspectives, values, beliefs, and points of view		X	X	X
Recognize and appreciate the diversity within and across First Peoples societies as represented in texts		X	X	X
Apply appropriate strategies in a variety of contexts to guide inquiry, extend thinking, and comprehend texts		X		X
Construct meaningful personal connections between self, text, and world	X	X	X	X
Think critically, creatively, and reflectively to explore ideas within, between, and beyond texts	X	X	X	X
Recognize and appreciate how different forms, structures, and features of texts reflect diverse purposes, audiences, and messages	X	X		X
Recognize the impact of personal, social, and cultural identities in First Peoples texts		X	X	X

6 Based on *BC's New Curriculum: English First Peoples Literary Studies 10*. Accessed October 8, 2019. https://curriculum.gov.bc.ca/curriculum/english-language-arts/10/efp-literary-studies

Examine how literary elements, techniques, and devices enhance and shape meaning and impact	X	X		X
Assess the authenticity of First Peoples texts		X		
Identify bias, contradictions, and distortions		X		
Respectfully exchange ideas and viewpoints from diverse perspectives to build shared understandings and extend thinking		X		X
Respond to text in personal, creative, and critical ways	X	X	X	X
Demonstrate speaking and listening skills in a variety of formal and informal contexts for a range of purposes		X		X
Recognize intellectual property rights and community protocols and apply them as necessary		X		
Use the conventions of First Peoples and other Canadian spelling, syntax, and diction proficiently and as appropriate to the context	X	X		X
Express an opinion and support it with evidence		X		X
Use writing and design processes to plan, develop, and create engaging and meaningful texts for a variety of purposes and audiences	X	X		X
Assess and refine texts to improve clarity and impact	X	X		X

Content
Students are expected to know the following:

Text forms and genres	X			
Common themes in First Peoples texts		X		
Reconciliation in Canada		X		X
First Peoples oral traditions • purposes of First Peoples oral text		X		
Protocols • protocols related to ownership and use of First Peoples oral texts		X		
Text features and structures • narrative structures, including those found in First Peoples texts • form, function, and genre of texts	X	X		

SURVIVING THE CITY TEACHER GUIDE © 2019 PORTAGE & MAIN PRESS ISBN: 978-1-55379-904-7

Content Students are expected to know the following:				
A wide variety of BC, Canadian, and global First Peoples texts	X	X		
A wide variety of text forms and genres	X	X		
Common themes in First Peoples texts	X	X		
Reconciliation in Canada		X		X
First Peoples oral traditions • the legal status of first peoples oral traditions in canada • purposes of oral texts • the relationship between oral tradition and land/place		X		
Protocols • protocols related to the ownership and use of First Peoples oral texts • acknowledgement of territory • situating oneself in relation to others and place • processes related to protocols and expectations when engaging with First Nations communities and Aboriginal organizations		X		
Text features and structures • narrative structures, including those found in FirstP eoples texts • form, function, and genre of oral and other texts	X	X		
Strategies and processes • reading strategies • oral language strategies • metacognitive strategies • writing processes • oral storytelling techniques • presentation and performance strategies	X	X	X	X
Language features, structures, and conventions • features of oral language • elements of style • syntax and fluency • rhetorical devices • usage and conventions • literary elements and devices • literal and inferential meaning • persuasive techniques • citations and acknowledgements	X	X	X	X

SURVIVING THE CITY TEACHER GUIDE © 2019 PORTAGE & MAIN PRESS ISBN: 978-1-55379-904-7

BRITISH COLUMBIA: ENGLISH FIRST PEOPLES 12

Curricular Competencies [8] Using oral, written, visual, and digital texts, students are expected individually and collaboratively to be able to:	Lesson			
	1	2	3	4
Analyze how First Peoples languages and texts reflect their cultures, knowledge, histories, and worldviews		X		
Access information for diverse purposes and from a variety of sources and evaluate its relevance, accuracy, and reliability		X	X	X
Select and apply appropriate strategies in a variety of contexts to guide inquiry, extend thinking, and comprehend texts	X	X	X	X
Analyze how different forms, formats, structures, and features of texts reflect a variety of purposes, audiences, and messages	X	X	X	X
Think critically, creatively, and reflectively to explore ideas within, between, and beyond texts	X	X	X	X
Recognize and identify personal, social, and cultural contexts, values, and perspectives in texts, including gender, sexual orientation, and socioeconomic factors		X	X	X
Appreciate and understand how language constructs and reflects personal, social, and cultural identities	X	X	X	X
Construct meaningful personal connections between self, text, and world	X	X	X	X
Demonstrate understanding of the role of story and oral traditions in expressing First Peoples perspectives, values, beliefs, and points of view		X		X
Understand and evaluate how literary elements, techniques, and devices enhance and shape meaning and impact	X	X		X
Analyze the diversity within and across First Peoples societies as represented in texts		X		X
Assess the authenticity of First Peoples texts		X		
Analyze the influence of land/place in First Peoples texts		X		X

8 Based on *BC's New Curriculum: English First Peoples 12*. Accessed October 8, 2019. https://curriculum.gov.bc.ca/curriculum/ english-language-arts/12/english-first-peoples

SURVIVING THE CITY TEACHER GUIDE © 2019 PORTAGE & MAIN PRESS   ISBN: 978-1-55379-904-7

Examine the significance of terms/words from First Peoples languages used in English texts		X		
Discern nuances in the meanings of words, considering social, political, historical, and literary contexts		X		
Identify bias, contradictions, distortions, and omissions		X		
Respectfully exchange ideas and viewpoints from diverse perspectives to build shared understandings and extend thinking		X		X
Demonstrate speaking and listening skills in a variety of formal and informal contexts for a range of purposes		X	X	X
Select and apply appropriate spoken language formats for intended purposes	X	X		X
Express and support an opinion with evidence	X	X		X
Respond to text in personal, creative, and critical ways	X	X	X	X
Use writing and design processes to plan, develop, and create engaging and meaningful texts for a variety of purposes and audiences	X	X		X
Assess and refine texts to improve clarity, effectiveness, and impact		X		X
Experiment with genres, forms, or styles of oral and other texts	X	X		X
Transform ideas and information to create original texts, using various genres, forms, structures, and styles	X	X		
Recognize intellectual property rights and community protocols and apply them as necessary		X		
Content Students are expected to know the following:				
A wide variety of BC, Canadian, and global First Peoples texts	X			
A wide variety of text forms and genres	X	X		
Common themes in First Peoples texts	X	X		
Reconciliation in Canada		X		X

SURVIVING THE CITY TEACHER GUIDE © 2019 PORTAGE & MAIN PRESS ISBN: 978-1-55379-904-7

First Peoples oral traditions • the legal status of First Peoples oral traditions in Canada • purposes of oral texts • the relationship between oral tradition and land/place	X		
Protocols • protocols related to the ownership and use of First Peoples oral texts • acknowledgement of territory • situating oneself in relation to others and place • processes related to protocols and expectations when engaging with First Nations communities and Aboriginal organizations	X		
Text features and structures • narrative structures, including those found in First Peoples texts • form, function, and genre of texts • elements of visual/graphic texts	X	X		
Strategies and processes • reading strategies • oral language strategies • metacognitive strategies • writing processes • presentation techniques	X	X	X	X
Language features, structures, and conventions • features of oral language • elements of style • language choice • syntax and sentence fluency • rhetorical devices • usage and conventions • literary elements and devices • literal and inferential meaning • persuasive techniques • citations and acknowledgements	X	X	X	X

SURVIVING THE CITY TEACHER GUIDE © 2019 PORTAGE & MAIN PRESS ISBN: 978-1-55379-904-7

MANITOBA: SENIOR 1 ENGLISH LANGUAGE ARTS

Curriculum Outcomes [9]	Lesson			
	1	**2**	**3**	**4**
1.1.1 Express Ideas Question and reflect on personal responses, predictions, and interpretations; apply personal viewpoints to diverse situations or circumstances.	X	X		X
1.1.2 Consider Others' Ideas Acknowledge the value of others' ideas and opinions in exploring and extending personal interpretations and viewpoints.	X	X	X	X
1.1.3 Experiment with Language and Form Use memorable language effectively and experiment with different personas for dynamic self-expression.	X	X		X
1.2.1 Develop Understanding Reflect on new understanding in relation to prior knowledge and identify gaps in personal knowledge.	X	X	X	X
1.2.2 Explain Opinions Review and refine personal viewpoints through reflection, feedback, and self-assessment.		X		X
1.2.4 Extend Understanding Consider diverse opinions, explore ambiguities, and assess whether new information clarifies understanding.		X		X
2.1.1 Prior Knowledge Analyze and explain connections between previous experiences, prior knowledge, and a variety of texts [including books].		X		X
2.1.2 Comprehension Strategies Use comprehension strategies [including recognizing main ideas and significant supporting details, and paraphrasing ideas] appropriate to the type of text and purpose; enhance understanding by rereading and discussing relevant passages.		X		X
2.1.3 Textual Cues Use textual cues and prominent organizational patterns within texts to construct and confirm meaning and interpret texts.	X	X		X

SURVIVING THE CITY TEACHER GUIDE © 2019 PORTAGE & MAIN PRESS ISBN: 978-1-55379-904-7

9 Based on the 1996 edition of *Senior 1 English Language Arts: Manitoba Curriculum Framework of Outcomes and Senior 1 Standards.*
https://www.edu.gov.mb.ca/k12/cur/ela/docs/s1_framework/index.html

2.2.2 Connect Self, Texts and Culture Examine how personal experiences, community traditions, and Canadian perspectives are presented in oral, literary, and media texts.	X	X	X	X
2.3.5 Create Original Texts Create original texts to communicate and demonstrate understanding of forms and techniques.	X	X	X	
3.1.3 Participate in Group Inquiry Generate and access ideas in a group and use a variety of methods to focus and clarify inquiry or research topic.		X		X
3.3.1 Organize Information Organize information and ideas by developing and selecting appropriate categories and organizational structures.	X	X	X	X
3.3.2 Record Information Summarize and record information in a variety of forms in own words, paraphrasing and/or quoting relevant facts and opinions; reference sources.	X	X		X
4.2.2. Revise Content Analyze and revise drafts to ensure appropriate content, accuracy, clarity, and completeness.	X	X	X	X
4.2.3 Enhance Legibility Use appropriate text features to enhance legibility for particular audiences, purposes, and contexts.	X	X		X
4.3.1 Grammar and Usage Edit for parallel structure, use of transitional devices, and clarity.	X	X		X
4.3.2 Spelling Know and apply a repertoire of spelling conventions when editing and proofreading; use a variety of resources when editing and proofreading.	X	X		X
4.3.3 Capitalization and Punctuation Know and apply capitalization and punctuation conventions in dialogues, quotations, footnotes, endnotes, and references when editing and proofreading.	X	X		X
4.4.2 Effective Oral Communication Choose vocabulary, voice production factors, and nonverbal cues to communicate effectively to a variety of audiences; use a variety of media and display techniques to enhance the effectiveness of oral presentations.		X		X
5.1.1 Cooperate with Others Recognize the importance of effective communication in working with others.				X

SURVIVING THE CITY TEACHER GUIDE © 2019 PORTAGE & MAIN PRESS   ISBN: 978-1-55379-904-7

	Lesson			
				X

5.1.2 Work in Groups Plan, organize, and participate in presentations of group finding.				X
5.2.1 Compare Responses Recognize that differing perspectives and unique reactions enrich understanding.	X	X		X

MANITOBA: SENIOR 2 ENGLISH LANGUAGE ARTS

Curriculum Outcomes [10]	Lesson			
	1	2	3	4
1.1.1 Express Ideas Consider the potential of emerging ideas through a variety of means to develop tentative positions.	X	X		X
1.1.3 Experiment with Language and Form Demonstrate a willingness to take risks in language use and experiment with language and forms of expression.	X	X		X
1.2.2 Explain Opinions Explain opinions, providing support or reasons; anticipate other viewpoints.		X		X
1.2.4 Extend Understanding Explore ways in which real and vicarious experiences and various perspectives affect understanding when generating and responding to texts.		X		X
2.1.1 Prior Knowledge Apply personal experiences and prior knowledge of language and texts to develop understanding and interpretations of a variety of texts [including books].	X	X	X	X
2.1.2 Comprehension Strategies Select, describe, and use comprehension strategies to monitor understanding and develop interpretations of a variety of texts.	X	X		X
2.1.3 Textual Cues Use textual cues and prominent organizational patterns to construct and confirm meaning and interpret texts.	X	X		X
2.2.2 Connect Self, Texts, and Culture Respond personally and critically to individuals, events, and ideas presented in a variety of Canadian and international texts.	X	X	X	X

SURVIVING THE CITY TEACHER GUIDE © 2019 PORTAGE & MAIN PRESS   ISBN: 978-1-55379-904-7

10   Based on the 1998 edition of *Senior 2 English Language Arts: Manitoba Curriculum Framework of Outcomes*. https://www.edu.gov.mb.ca/k12/cur/ela/docs/s2_framework/index.html

2.3.5 Create Original Texts Create original texts to communicate ideas and enhance understanding of forms and techniques.	X	X	X	
3.1.3 Participate in Group Inquiry Collaborate to determine group knowledge base and to define research or inquiry purpose and parameters.				X
3.3.1 Organize Information Organize information using appropriate forms for specific purposes.	X	X	X	X
3.3.2 Record Information Select and record important information and ideas using an organizational structure appropriate for purpose and information source; document sources accurately.	X	X	X	X
4.2.2 Revise Content Analyze and revise drafts to ensure appropriate content, accuracy, clarity, and completeness.	X	X	X	X
4.2.3 Enhance Legibility Use appropriate text features to enhance legibility for particular audiences, purposes, and contexts.	X	X		X
4.3.1 Grammar and Usage Select appropriate words, grammatical structures, and register to achieve clarity and desired effect.	X	X		X
4.3.2 Spelling Know and apply Canadian spelling conventions for familiar and new vocabulary; monitor for correctness in editing and proofreading using appropriate resources.	X	X		X
4.3.3 Capitalization and Punctuation Know and apply capitalization and punctuation conventions to clarify intended meaning, using appropriate resources as required.	X	X		X
4.4.2 Effective Oral Communication Use appropriate voice production factors and non-verbal cues to clarify intent in personal and public communication.		X		X
5.1.1 Cooperate with Others Make and encourage contributions to assist in developing group ideas; take responsibility for developing and expressing viewpoints.				X
5.1.2 Work in Groups Demonstrate effective group interaction skills and strategies.				X
5.2.1 Compare Responses Consider various ideas, evidence, and viewpoints to expand understanding of texts, others, and self.	X	X		X

SURVIVING THE CITY TEACHER GUIDE © 2019 PORTAGE & MAIN PRESS ISBN: 978-1-55379-904-7

MANITOBA: SENIOR 3 ENGLISH LANGUAGE ARTS

Curriculum Outcomes [11]	Lesson			
	1	**2**	**3**	**4**
1.1.1 Express Ideas Connect ideas, observations, opinions, and emotions through a variety of means to develop a train of thought and test tentative positions.	X	X	X	X
1.1.3 Experiment with Language and Form Experiment with language and forms of expression to achieve particular effects.	X	X		X
1.2.2 Explain Opinions Explore various viewpoints and consider the consequences of particular positions when generating and responding to texts.		X		X
1.2.4 Extend Understanding Extend understanding by exploring and acknowledging multiple perspectives and ambiguities when generating and responding to texts.		X		X
2.1.1 Prior Knowledge Examine connections between personal experiences and prior knowledge of language and texts to develop understanding and interpretations of a variety of texts [including books].	X	X		X
2.1.2 Comprehension Strategies Use and adjust comprehension strategies to monitor understanding and develop interpretations of a variety of texts.	X	X		X
2.1.3 Textual Cues Use textual cues and prominent organizational patterns to construct and confirm meaning and interpret texts.	X	X		X
2.2.2 Connect Self, Texts, and Culture Respond personally and critically to ideas and values presented in a variety of Canadian and international texts.	X	X	X	X
2.3.5 Create Original Texts Create original texts to communicate ideas and enhance understanding of forms and techniques.	X	X		X

SURVIVING THE CITY TEACHER GUIDE © 2019 PORTAGE & MAIN PRESS ISBN: 978-1-55379-904-7

11 Based on the 1999 edition of *Senior 3 English Language Arts: Manitoba Curriculum Framework of Outcomes.* https://www.edu.gov.mb.ca/k12/cur/ela/docs/s3_framework/index.html

3.1.3 Participate in Group Inquiry Explore group knowledge and strengths to determine inquiry or research topic, purpose, and procedures.				X
3.3.1 Organize Information Organize and reorganize information and ideas in a variety of ways for different audiences and purposes.	X	X		X
3.3.2 Record Information Summarize and record information, ideas, and perspectives from a variety of sources; document sources accurately.	X	X		X
4.2.2 Revise Content Analyze and revise drafts to ensure appropriate content and to enhance unity, clarity, and coherence.	X	X		X
4.2.3 Enhance Legibility Use appropriate text features to enhance legibility for particular audiences, purposes, and contexts.	X	X		X
4.3.1 Grammar and Usage Select appropriate words, grammatical structures, and register for audience, purpose, and context.	X	X		X
4.3.2 Spelling Know and apply Canadian spelling conventions and monitor for correctness using appropriate resources; recognize adapted spellings for particular effects.	X	X		X
4.3.3 Capitalization and Punctuation Know and apply capitalization and punctuation conventions to clarify intended meaning, using appropriate resources as required.	X	X		X
4.4.2 Effective Oral and Visual Communication Use appropriate voice and visual production factors to communicate and emphasize intent in personal and public communication.	X	X		X
5.1.1 Cooperate with Others Use language to build and maintain collaborative relationships; take responsibility for respectfully questioning others' viewpoints and requesting further explanation.				X
5.1.2 Work in Groups Demonstrate flexibility in assuming a variety of group roles and take responsibility for tasks that achieve group goals.				X
5.2.1 Compare Responses Identify various factors that shape understanding of texts, others, and self.	X	X		X

SURVIVING THE CITY TEACHER GUIDE © 2019 PORTAGE & MAIN PRESS ISBN: 978-1-55379-904-7

MANITOBA: SENIOR 4 ENGLISH LANGUAGE ARTS

Curriculum Outcomes [12]	Lesson			
	1	**2**	**3**	**4**
1.1.1 Express Ideas Connect ideas, observations, opinions, and emotions through a variety of means to develop a train of thought and test tentative positions.	X	X		X
1.1.3 Experiment with Language and Form Experiment with language and forms of expression to achieve particular effects.	X	X		X
1.2.2 Explain Opinions Explore various viewpoints and consider the consequences of particular positions when generating and responding to texts.	X	X		X
1.2.4 Extend Understanding Extend understanding by exploring and acknowledging multiple perspectives and ambiguities when generating and responding to texts.	X	X		X
2.1.1 Prior Knowledge Examine connections between personal experiences and prior knowledge of language and texts to develop understanding and interpretations of a variety of texts [including books].	X	X	X	X
2.1.2 Comprehension Strategies Use and adjust comprehension strategies to monitor understanding and develop interpretations of a variety of texts.	X	X		X
2.1.3 Textual Cues Use textual cues and prominent organizational patterns to construct and confirm meaning and interpret texts.	X	X		X
2.2.2 Connect Self, Texts, and Culture Respond personally and critically to ideas and values presented in a variety of Canadian and international texts.	X	X	X	X
2.3.5 Create Original Texts Create original texts to communicate ideas and enhance understanding of forms and techniques.	X	X		X

SURVIVING THE CITY TEACHER GUIDE © 2019 PORTAGE & MAIN PRESS ISBN: 978-1-55379-904-7

12 Based on the 2000 edition of *Senior 4 English Language Arts: Manitoba Curriculum Framework of Outcomes and Senior 4 Standards*.
https://www.edu.gov.mb.ca/k12/cur/ela/docs/s4_framework/index.html

3.1.3 Participate in Group Inquiry Explore group knowledge and strengths to determine inquiry or research topic, purpose, and procedures.				X
3.3.1 Organize Information Organize and reorganize information and ideas in a variety of ways for different audiences and purposes.	X	X		X
3.3.2 Record Information Summarize and record information, ideas, and perspectives from a variety of sources; document sources accurately.	X	X		X
4.2.2 Revise Content Analyze and revise drafts to ensure appropriate content and to enhance unity, clarity, and coherence.	X	X	X	X
4.2.3 Enhance Legibility Use appropriate text features to enhance legibility for particular audiences, purposes, and contexts.	X	X		X
4.3.1 Grammar and Usage Select appropriate words, grammatical structures, and register for audience, purpose, and context.	X	X		X
4.3.2 Spelling Know and apply Canadian spelling conventions and monitor for correctness using appropriate resources; recognize adapted spellings for particular effects.	X	X		X
4.3.3 Capitalization and Punctuation Know and apply capitalization and punctuation conventions to clarify intended meaning, using appropriate resources as required.	X	X		X
4.4.2 Effective Oral and Visual Communication Use appropriate voice and visual production factors to communicate and emphasize intent in personal and public communication.	X	X		X
5.1.1 Cooperate with Others Use language to build and maintain collaborative relationships; take responsibility for respectfully questioning others' viewpoints and requesting further explanation.		X		X
5.1.2 Work in Groups Demonstrate flexibility in assuming a variety of group roles and take responsibility for tasks that achieve group goals.				X
5.2.1 Compare Responses Identify various factors that shape understanding of texts, others, and self.				X

SURVIVING THE CITY TEACHER GUIDE © 2019 PORTAGE & MAIN PRESS ISBN:978-1-55379-904-7

MANITOBA: GRADE 12 GLOBAL ISSUES: CITIZENSHIP AND SUSTAINABILITY

Curriculum Outcomes [13]	Lesson			
	1	**2**	**3**	**4**
Learning to Know *Acquire knowledge and understanding, and think critically about our complex and changing world.*				
Seek knowledge from diverse sources and perspectives.				X
Conduct focused in-depth inquiry.				X
Learning to Do *Learn to participate effectively in local, national, and global communities.*				
Engage in intercultural dialogue and cultivate a widening circle of empathy and concern.				X
Take Action				
Explore Indigenous perspectives to extend the boundaries of the familiar and to challenge assumptions and practices.				X
Area of Inquiry: Indigenous Peoples				
Inquire about the legacy of colonialism, colonization, and decolonization.				X
Inquire about the effects of enculturation, assimilation, and cultural loss for Indigenous Peoples.				X
Inquire about the impact of development and globalization on Indigenous Peoples, cultural homogenization, and the disappearance of Indigenous Peoples and cultures.				X
Inquire about the preservation of traditional Indigenous cultures and languages.				X
Inquire about the recognition of distinctive Indigenous worldviews and values.				X

SURVIVING THE CITY TEACHER GUIDE © 2019 PORTAGE & MAIN PRESS ISBN: 978-1-55379-904-7

13 Based on the 2017 edition of *Grade 12 Global Issues: Citizenship and Sustainability*. https://www.edu.gov.mb.ca/k12/cur/socstud/global_issues/index.html

MANITOBA:
GRADE 12 CURRENT TOPICS IN FIRST NATIONS, MÉTIS, AND INUIT STUDIES

Curriculum Outcomes [14]	Lesson			
	1	2	3	4
1.1 Learn about the colonialist history of Canada and the impact of colonization on First Nations, Métis, and Inuit peoples in Canada.				X
1.2 Explore Indigenous identity from the viewpoint of First Nations, Métis, and Inuit peoples.		X	X	X
1.3 Examine contemporary mainstream Canadian society's perception of Indigenous people as "the other."				X
2.1 Investigate the historic, political, and economic practices of Indigenous peoples in Canada, before and after the arrival of Europeans.				X
2.3 Examine the historic and contemporary significance of the Indian act, including the paradox that it is at once discriminatory and racist while it also preserves the sanctity of reserve lands.				X
3.3 Examine traditional Indigenous concepts and practices of justice, as well as the impact of colonization and the imposition of a western judicial model on First Nations, Metis, and Inuit peoples.				X
5.1 Work independently as individuals or with a partner or small group to create a project focusing on a theme relevant to contemporary Indigenous culture.				X

SURVIVING THE CITY TEACHER GUIDE © 2019 PORTAGE & MAIN PRESS ISBN: 978-1-55379-904-7

14 Based on the 2011 edition of *Grade 12 Current Topics in First Nations, Métis, and Inuit Studies: A Foundation for Implementation.*
https://www.edu.gov.mb.ca/k12/abedu/foundation_gr12/full_doc.pdf

ONTARIO: GRADE 9 ENGLISH LANGUAGE ARTS (ACADEMIC)

Curriculum Outcomes [15]	Lesson			
	1	2	3	4
Writing **Developing and Organizing Content** By the end of this course, students will:				
1.2 generate and focus ideas for potential writing tasks, using several different strategies and print, electronic, and other resources, as appropriate	X		X	X
1.3 locate and select information to support ideas for writing, using several different strategies and print, electronic, and other resources, as appropriate		X		X
1.4 identify, sort, and order main ideas and supporting details for writing tasks, using several different strategies and organizational patterns suited to the content and purpose for writing	X	X		X
Writing **Using Knowledge of Form and Style** By the end of this course, students will:				
2.4 write complete sentences that communicate their meaning clearly and accurately, varying sentence type, structure, and length for different purposes and making logical transitions between ideas	X	X		X
2.6 revise drafts to improve the content, organization, clarity, and style of their written work, using a variety of teacher-modelled strategies	X	X		X
Writing **Applying Knowledge of Conventions** By the end of this course, students will:				
3.5 proofread and correct their writing, using guidelines developed with the teacher and peers	X	X		X

SURVIVING THE CITY TEACHER GUIDE © 2019 PORTAGE & MAIN PRESS ISBN: 978-1-55379-904-7

15 Based on the 2007 edition of *The Ontario Curriculum, Grades 9 and 10: English.* http://www.edu.gov.on.ca/eng/curriculum/secondary/english910currb.pdf

Oral Communication
Speaking to Communicate
By the end of this course, students will:

2.1 communicate orally for several different purposes, using language suitable for the intended audience		X		X
2.2 demonstrate an understanding of several different interpersonal speaking strategies and adapt them to suit the purpose, situation, and audience, exhibiting sensitivity to cultural differences		X		X
2.3 communicate in a clear, coherent manner appropriate to the purpose, subject matter, and intended audience		X		X

Reading and Literature Studies
Understanding Form and Style
By the end of this course, students will:

2.1 identify several different characteristics of literary, informational, and graphic text forms and explain how they help communicate meaning	X	X		X
2.2 identify several different text features and explain how they help communicate meaning	X			

SURVIVING THE CITY TEACHER GUIDE © 2019 PORTAGE & MAIN PRESS ISBN: 978-1-55379-904-7

ONTARIO: GRADE 10 ENGLISH LANGUAGE ARTS (ACADEMIC)

Curriculum Outcomes [16]	Lesson			
	1	2	3	4
Listen to Understand By the end of this course, students will:				
1.2 select and use appropriate active listening strategies when participating in a variety of classroom interactions	X	X	X	X
Speaking to Communicate By the end of this course, students will:				
2.1 communicate orally for a variety of purposes, using language appropriate for the intended audience		X		X
2.2 demonstrate an understanding of a variety of interpersonal speaking strategies and adapt them to suit the purpose, situation, and audience, exhibiting sensitivity to cultural difference		X		X
2.3 communicate in a clear, coherent manner, using a structure and style appropriate to the purpose, subject matter, and intended audience		X		X

ONTARIO: GRADE 11 ENGLISH LANGUAGE ARTS (UNIVERSITY PREP)

Curriculum Outcomes [17]	Lesson			
	1	2	3	4
Developing and Organizing Content By the end of this course, students will:				
1.2 generate and focus ideas for potential writing tasks, using several different strategies and print, electronic, and other resources, as appropriate	X	X		X
1.3 locate and select information to support ideas for writing, using several different strategies and print, electronic, and other resources, as appropriate		X		X
1.4 identify, sort, and order main ideas and supporting details for writing tasks, using several different strategies and organizational patterns suited to the content and purpose for writing		X		X

SURVIVING THE CITY TEACHER GUIDE © 2019 PORTAGE & MAIN PRESS ISBN: 978-1-55379-904-7

16 Based on the 2007 edition of *The Ontario Curriculum, Grades 9 and 10: English.* http://www.edu.gov.on.ca/eng/curriculum/secondary/english910currb.pdf

17 Based on the 2007 edition of *The Ontario Curriculum, Grades 11 and 12: English.* http://www.edu.gov.on.ca/eng/curriculum/secondary/english1112currb.pdf

Speaking to Communicate By the end of this course, students will:				
2.1 communicate orally for several different purposes, using language suitable for the intended audience		X		X
2.2 demonstrate an understanding of a variety of interpersonal speaking strategies and adapt them to suit the purpose, situation, and audience, exhibiting sensitivity to cultural differences		X		X
2.3 communicate in a clear, coherent manner, using a structure and style effective for the purpose, subject matter, and intended audience		X		X

ONTARIO: GRADE 11 ENGLISH LANGUAGE ARTS (READING AND LITERATURE STUDIES)

Curriculum Outcomes [18]	Lesson			
	1	**2**	**3**	**4**
Reading for Meaning By the end of this course, students will:				
1.5 extend understanding of texts, including increasingly complex or difficult texts, by making appropriate and increasingly rich connections between the ideas in them and personal knowledge, experience, and insights; other texts; and the world around them		X		X
1.8 identify and analyze the perspectives and/or biases evident in texts, including increasingly complex or difficult texts, commenting with growing understanding on any questions they may raise about beliefs, values, identity, and power		X		
Understanding Form and Style By the end of this course, students will:				
2.1 identify a variety of characteristics of literary, informational, and graphic text forms and explain how they help communicate meaning	X			
Reading with Fluency By the end of this course, students will:				
3.5 proofread and correct their writing, using guidelines developed with the teacher and peers	X	X		

SURVIVING THE CITY TEACHER GUIDE © 2019 PORTAGE & MAIN PRESS ISBN: 978-1-55379-904-7

---

18 Based on the 2007 edition of *The Ontario Curriculum, Grades 11 and 12: English*. http://www.edu.gov.on.ca/eng/curriculum/secondary/english1112currb.pdf

ONTARIO: GRADE 12 ENGLISH LANGUAGE ARTS (UNIVERSITY PREP)

Curriculum Outcomes [19]	Lesson			
	1	2	3	4
Oral Communication By the end of this course, students will:				
1.1 identify the purpose of a wide range of listening tasks and set goals for specific tasks	X	X	X	X
Speaking to Communicate By the end of this course, students will:				
2.1 communicate orally for a wide range of purposes, using language effective for the intended audience	X	X		X
2.2 demonstrate an understanding of a variety of interpersonal speaking strategies and adapt them to suit the purpose, situation, and audience, exhibiting sensitivity to cultural differences	X	X	X	X
2.3 communicate in a clear, coherent manner, using a structure and style effective for the purpose, subject matter, and intended audience	X	X		X

ONTARIO: GRADE 12 ENGLISH LANGUAGE ARTS (READING AND LITERATURE STUDIES)

Curriculum Outcomes [20]	Lesson			
	1	2	3	4
Reading for Meaning By the end of this course, students will:				
1.5 extend understanding of texts, including complex and challenging texts, by making rich and increasingly insightful connections between the ideas in them and personal knowledge, experience, and insights; other texts; and the world around them	X			X

SURVIVING THE CITY TEACHER GUIDE © 2019 PORTAGE & MAIN PRESS ISBN: 978-1-55379-904-7

19 Based on the 2007 edition of *The Ontario Curriculum, Grades 11 and 12: English.* http://www.edu.gov.on.ca/eng/curriculum/secondary/english1112currb.pdf

20 Based on the 2007 edition of *The Ontario Curriculum, Grades 11 and 12: English.* http://www.edu.gov.on.ca/eng/curriculum/secondary/english1112currb.pdf

	1	2	3	4
1.8 identify and analyze the perspectives and/or biases evident in texts, including complex and challenging texts, commenting with understanding and increasing insight on any questions they may raise about beliefs, values, identity, and power		X		X
Understanding Form and Style By the end of this course, students will:				
2.1 identify a variety of characteristics of literary, informational, and graphic text forms and demonstrate insight into the way they help communicate meaning	X			
Reading with Fluency by the end of this course, students will:				
3.5 proofread and correct their writing, using guidelines developed with the teacher and peers	X	X	X	X

ONTARIO: GRADE 11 AND 12 FIRST NATIONS, MÉTIS, AND INUIT STUDIES

Curriculum Outcomes [21]	Lesson			
	1	2	3	4
Identity				
Overall Expectations By the end of this course, students will:				
Describe the concepts related to identity in Aboriginal literary works		X		
Analyze and assess information, ideas, issues, and language as they pertain to Aboriginal identity in a variety of informational writings and Aboriginal literary works		X		
Demonstrate an understanding of how the different forms and styles used in Aboriginal literary works reflect Aboriginal identity		X		
Analyze images in media works related to Aboriginal identity		X		
Specific Expectations: Aboriginal Voices in Literature By the end of this course, students will:				
Identify the perceptions of Aboriginal identity expressed by a variety of Aboriginal writers		X	X	X

SURVIVING THE CITY TEACHER GUIDE © 2019 PORTAGE & MAIN PRESS ISBN: 978-1-55379-904-7

21 Based on the 2007 edition of *The Ontario Curriculum, Grades 11 and 12: English.* http://www.edu.gov.on.ca/eng/curriculum/secondary/english1112currb.pdf

Assess Aboriginal writers' depictions of aspects of Aboriginal identity that have resulted from interactions with Canadian society		X	X	X
Explain social and historical values and perspectives on Aboriginal identity, based on examples from Aboriginal literature		X	X	X

Specific Expectations: Language
By the end of this course, students will:

Explain how literature provides telling insights into the character and ways of a people		X	X	X

Relationships

Overall Expectations
By the end of this course, students will:

Demonstrate an understanding of relationships (e.g., within the family or community; within the plant, animal, or spirit world) portrayed in the works of Aboriginal writers		X	X	X
Demonstrate an understanding of the ways in which Aboriginal writers depict relationships to promote a vision of Aboriginal communities		X		
Demonstrate an understanding of form, purpose, audience, and production techniques by designing or creating media works, independently and collaboratively, based on the ideas, themes, and issues related to relationships examined in this course	X	X		X
Compare, through analysis, relationships presented in media works by Aboriginal creators		X		

Specific Expectations: Aboriginal Voices in Media Works
By the end of this course, students will:

Compare the ways in which different Aboriginal communities work to restore relationships and values, as depicted in media works by Aboriginal creators		X	X	X

SURVIVING THE CITY TEACHER GUIDE © 2019 PORTAGE & MAIN PRESS ISBN: 978-1-55379-904-7

Sovereignty

Specific Expectations: Aboriginal Voices in Media Works
By the end of this course, students will:

Identify the role and importance of sovereignty in contemporary Aboriginal communities, as portrayed by Aboriginal writers		X	X	X

Challenges

Specific Expectations: Aboriginal Voices in Media Works
By the end of this course, students will:

Analyze Aboriginal writers' depictions of challenges faced by Aboriginal peoples that have resulted directly from societal influences (e.g., racism, ethnocentricity, marginalization)		X	X	X
Analyze efforts made by Aboriginal peoples to respond to challenges, as portrayed in the works of Aboriginal writers		X	X	X

Writing

Specific Expectations: Choosing the Form to Suit the Purpose and Audience
By the end of this course, students will:

Demonstrate an understanding of the uses and conventions of a variety of forms by writing persuasive and literary essays, reviews, short narratives or poems, and summaries		X		X

Specific Expectations: Revising Drafts
By the end of this course, students will:

Revise drafts to strengthen content and improve organization by refining the controlling idea		X		X

Specific Expectations: Editing, Proofreading, and Publishing
By the end of this course, students will:

Edit and proofread their own and others' writing, identifying and correcting errors according to the requirements for grammar, usage, spelling, and punctuation	X	X		X

SURVIVING THE CITY TEACHER GUIDE © 2019 PORTAGE & MAIN PRESS ISBN: 978-1-55379-904-7

SURVIVING THE CITY TEACHER GUIDE © 2019 PORTAGE & MAIN PRESS ISBN: 978-1-55379-904-7

LESSON 1

HOW DO WE READ GRAPHIC NOVELS?

DURATION

One hour

OVERVIEW

Graphic novels (and comics) are a unique format of literature that includes many parts. This lesson is designed to introduce teachers and students alike to the unique features of this format. Throughout the lesson, students will research the parts of a graphic novel and then create their own graphic novel scene incorporating these parts.

BACKGROUND

The terms *graphic novel* and *comic book* describe the format of a book, rather than a genre. Graphic novels and comic books can be fiction, nonfiction, biography, fantasy, dystopia, or any genre in between.[22] Graphic novels are an accessible reading resource for all students, and they have been proven to engage even the most reluctant of readers.[23] Graphic novels also include dialogue, characters' thoughts, narration, and captions. Graphic novels are meant to be read from left to right and top to bottom.

---

22 "What is a Graphic Novel?" Get Graphic, the Buffalo and Erie County Public Library and Partnering Organizations, accessed August 1, 2019, https://www.buffalolib.org/content/get-graphic/what-graphic-novel.

23 Knutson, Sarah. "How Graphic Novels Help Students Develop Critical Skills," Room 241: A Blog by Concordia University-Portland, updated October 23, 2018, https://education.cu-portland.edu/blog/classroom-resources/graphic-novels-visual-literacy/.

MATERIALS

- writing utensils
- whiteboard or chart paper
- markers
- pencil crayons
- Activity Sheet: All About Graphic Novels (1.1) (one copy for each student)
- Rubric: Graphic Novel Scene (1.2) (two copies for each student)
- computers/tablets with access to the internet (optional)
- art paper (one sheet for each student)

ACTIVATE: BRAINSTORM

Ask students what graphic novels or comic books they have read in the past. Make a list of these titles on a whiteboard or a piece of chart paper. Follow this brainstorm with a list of the parts of a comic with which students are already familiar (e.g., captions, sound effects, thought balloons).

ACQUIRE: FILL IN THE ACTIVITY SHEET: ALL ABOUT GRAPHIC NOVELS

Give each student a copy of the Activity Sheet: All About Graphic Novels (1.1). As you read the worksheet, have students fill in the missing words. Another option is to have students research and record the missing words as a "scavenger hunt" activity, using online and print sources.

Alternatively, have students create their own template to record the parts of a graphic novel.

Answer Key for Activity Sheet: All About Graphic Novels (1.1):

(1) gutters

(2) a visual or implied boundary, and the contents within it, that tell a piece of the story

(3) the space between the panels; as the reader moves from one panel to the next, they predict and conclude what is happening

(4) gutters

(5) change

(6) description

(7) focus on a character's thoughts and ideas

(8) focus on conversation between characters

(9) use texts of images to convey sound in a story

(10) dialogue

(11) narration

(12) motion

(13) moving

(14) realistic

(15) expressions

SURVIVING THE CITY TEACHER GUIDE © 2019 PORTAGE & MAIN PRESS   ISBN: 978-1-55379-904-7

APPLY: CREATE YOUR OWN GRAPHIC NOVEL SCENE

Explain to students that they will now create their own graphic novel scene. The scene can be an event from their day, for example, their commute to school, or an account of an after-school activity.

Before they begin, have students plan out their scenes. Students should write a brief description of the scene they would like to draw for each panel. Once they have each of their scenes planned (e.g., panel one: wake up in bed, panel two: brush teeth, panel three: eat breakfast, panel four: walk to school), have students write the dialogue, thoughts, and other elements that they want to include. Students should aim to incorporate at least four of the different parts of a graphic novel discussed in the Acquire activity. Have each student fold a sheet of paper in half and in half again, so they have four panels (boxes) on each side to use for their graphic novel scene. Have students use their descriptions to sketch a rough draft of their scene in the panels they have created.

ASSESS: PEER ASSESSMENT AND GRAPHIC NOVEL SCENE RUBRIC

Before students submit their graphic novel scenes, have them engage in a peer editing session. Distribute one copy of the Rubric: Graphic Novel Scene (1.2) to each student, and have students exchange their graphic novel scene with a partner. Have students review their partner's scene several times, and circle the level of proficiency they would give the student. Make sure students write an explanation for the grade they gave each category, using the back of the rubric to jot down their comments and suggestions for improvement. Remind students that constructive criticism is not personal and should include both positive comments and comments that suggest in a friendly manner an area needing improvement.

Have students revise their work and create a final draft on a fresh piece of paper before submitting the graphic novel scenes for final grading. Use the Rubric: Graphic Novel Scene (1.2) to assess students.

Date: _____   Name: _____

ALL ABOUT GRAPHIC NOVELS

When reading a graphic novel, it's important to understand all of the elements that make up a graphic novel. Fill in the blanks as instructed below.

Panels and _____(1)
Define the following terms.

Panel: _____

_____(2)

Gutter: _____

_____(3)

Fill in the blanks below to complete the sentences.

Consider the size and shape of panels. How do they fit together? Do they interrupt or overlap each other? Are there any images without panel borders at all? The spaces in between the panels— the _____(4)—indicate a _____(5): in how time is passing, in where you are, or at which character you're looking at or talking to. What do the gutters add to how you understand the story?

SURVIVING THE CITY TEACHER GUIDE © 2019 PORTAGE & MAIN PRESS   ISBN: 978-1-55379-904-7

1.1

Date: _____   Name: _____

ALL ABOUT GRAPHIC NOVELS

Define the following terms.

_____(6) AND WORD BALLOONS

Thought Balloon: _____

_____(7)

Dialogue Balloon: _____

_____(8)

Sound Effect Balloon: _____

_____(9)

Fill in the blanks below to complete the sentences.

Think about how the _____ (10) appears. Are the words different colours? Written with thicker or thinner lines? How would that sound? How about the silence when no one is speaking? Is there any _____ (11) or description (words in boxes, but not spoken)? How is that important to how the story unfolds?

SOUND EFFECTS AND _____ (12) LINES
Sounds set the scene, signal something off-scene, and add another layer to each story. Motion lines indicate how characters or objects are _____ (13). What sounds do you see? How are each of the sounds written—does the way it's written reflect what it actually sounds like? What gestures do you see?

ART
Every creator has their own style. Is the art _____ (14)? Cartoony? What can you tell from the _____ (15) on faces? The gestures and movement of characters? The background and its details? If there is color, how does that change over the course of a page? Each chapter?

SURVIVING THE CITY TEACHER GUIDE © 2019 PORTAGE & MAIN PRESS   ISBN: 978-1-55379-904-7

1.1

Date: _____   Name: _____

GRAPHIC NOVEL SCENE

CATEGORY	Excellent	Good	Developing/Needs Improvement
Comic Story Structure /10	The story/summary is very well-organized. One idea or scene follows another in a logical sequence with clear transitions.	The story/summary is pretty well-organized. One idea or scene may seem out of place. Clear transitions are used.	The story/summary is hard to follow. The transitions are sometimes not clear.
Visual Appeal /10	Carefully chosen images help the reader understand the action and emotions in the story/summary.	Most of the images help the reader understand the story. One or two are unrelated or confusing.	Comic includes many images that do not relate to the story and confuse readers.
Grammar & Spelling Conventions) /5	Writer makes no errors in grammar or spelling that distract the reader from the content in the graphic novel scene.	Writer makes a few errors in grammar or spelling that distract the reader from the content in the graphic novel scene.	Writer makes many errors in grammar or spelling that distract the reader from the content in the graphic novel scene.
Effort /5	Final product is completed and pride in one's work, proper time management, and adequate planning is evident.	Final product is short, and more effort could have been put into time management and/or adequate planning.	Final product is incomplete—pride in one's work, proper time management, and/or adequate planning is not evident.

Mark out of 30:

Comments:

SURVIVING THE CITY TEACHER GUIDE © 2019 PORTAGE & MAIN PRESS ISBN: 978-1-55379-904-7

1.2

LESSON 2

WHY IS CULTURE IMPORTANT?

DURATION

One to two hours

OVERVIEW

Throughout this lesson, students will learn about an aspect of Anishinaabe culture—the Berry Fast mentioned in *Surviving the City*. Students will then have an opportunity to research and share something from their own cultures.

BACKGROUND

Culture is an important aspect of identity formation. Culture includes many seen and unseen aspects of a group or society, including clothing, food, language, folklore/stories, literature, gender roles, humour, approaches to medicine and health, rules of conduct, pride, concept of justice, notions of modesty, and attitude towards the environment.

MATERIALS

- projector for presentations
- access to computers/tablets with slide show software
- Rubric: Oral Presentation (2.1) (two copies for each student)

ACTIVATE: THINK/PAIR/SHARE

Have students turn to a partner and discuss how they would define the word *culture*.

Solicit responses from the groups and, as a class, co-create a definition of culture that includes language, traditions, social norms, art, and values. Write this definition on the board for students to refer back to throughout the lesson.

Next, ask students to turn to their partners again and name things that are influenced by culture (e.g., clothing, food, language, stories, celebrations).

Solicit oral responses from the groups.

Discuss with students that culture is a complex term that includes many seen and unseen parts. Some things that we can see include: clothing, jewellery, food, language, folklore/stories, literature, holidays, and festivals.

Some unseen parts include: family roles, beliefs and assumptions, self-concept, relation to authority, core values, biases, body language, manners, beauty ideals, attitudes toward school, family values, gender roles, humour, approaches to medicine and health, rules of conduct, pride, concept of justice, notions of modesty, attitude towards the environment, competitiveness, expectations, child-rearing practices, gestures, and even personal space.

Ask the class if anyone knows what *cultural appropriation* is. Solicit responses from the groups. Ask students if they can give some examples of cultural appropriation. Examples might include non-Indigenous clothing designers copying traditional Indigenous designs for their clothing and selling it for a profit. Next, explain that Canadian copyright law protects Indigenous knowledge, including traditional cultural expressions.[24] This means that it is illegal to profit off of the culture of Indigenous Peoples in Canada. However, there are some grey areas—for example, some oral stories may be difficult to protect. Discuss with students that it is generally considered wrong to profit off of a culture that is not your own.

Ask the class to consider the following questions:

- Is *Surviving the City* considered an authentic Indigenous text? Why? (Yes because the author identifies as Nehiyaw and Trinidadian and is writing from an Indigenous perspective. Authentic texts present authentic Indigenous voices, depict themes and issues important to Indigenous peoples, and include respectful portrayals or representations of Indigenous peoples and their traditions and beliefs.)

SURVIVING THE CITY TEACHER GUIDE © 2019 PORTAGE & MAIN PRESS ISBN: 978-1-55379-904-7

---

24 Innovation, Science and Economic Development Canada. "Indigenous Peoples and Intellectual Property." Accessed October 1, 2019. https://www.ic.gc.ca/eic/site/108.nsf/eng/00004.html

- What are some of the themes in *Surviving the City*? (Indigenous topics such as the effects of genocide and intergenerational trauma, the harmful legacy of the residential school system, Missing and Murdered Indigenous Women and Girls and Two-Spirit people, the importance of ceremony in fostering resilience; the importance of friendship and family)

- What can *Surviving the City* teach us about reconciliation? (there is still a long way to go before reconciliation will be achieved; highlights ways we can begin to heal our own communities by loving each other, attending ceremony, and fighting for our rights)

Next, explain to students that they are going to explore the significance of culture for Indigenous peoples and for themselves.

ACQUIRE: ORAL STORYTELLING

Have students help you invite an Elder or Knowledge Keeper to speak to students about rites of passage in their communities. See Inviting an Elder Into Your Learning Space on page 4 for guidelines for inviting an Elder or Knowledge Keeper to your class,.

In addition (or as an alternative), read students the article "My Berry Fast" by Akeesha Footman from *Muskrat Magazine*: <http://muskratmagazine.com/my-berry-fast/>. The Berry Fast ceremony featured in *Surviving the City* is part of Anishinaabe (also known as Ojibwe) culture.

Depending on the time allotment, the next section might fit into a different class. Ensure students have a chance to talk and debrief with the Elder or discuss their thoughts on the article before the end of the first class.

To review, conduct a class discussion and ask the following questions to ensure comprehension and understanding:

Discussion Questions:
1. What is the purpose of a Berry Fast?
2. Why is a Berry Fast important?
3. What life lessons does it help teach?
4. How is the Berry Fast presented in *Surviving the City*?
5. Why do you think the author included the Berry Fast in *Surviving the City*?

APPLY: MY CULTURE ORAL PRESENTATION ASSIGNMENT

Explain to students that they will now have the opportunity to reflect on and teach the class about something important from their culture. Distribute one copy of the Rubric: Oral Presentation (2.1) to each student. Explain that their oral presentations must be accompanied by a slide show and should answer the following questions:

1. Describe the cultural activity.
2. What is the history of this activity?
3. How is this activity celebrated in the present day?
4. What important lessons does this activity teach?
5. What is your personal experience with this activity?

Allow students time to reflect on an aspect of their culture that they would like to share. Have students interview family members and conduct research to find answers to their questions.

Students' presentations should be about 3–5 minutes long. Encourage students to show pictures throughout.

ASSESS: PEER EDITING AND PRESENTATION RUBRIC

Before students present, have them engage in a peer-editing session. Distribute a copy of the Rubric: Oral Presentation (2.1) to each student, and have students pair up and practise their presentations with their partner. Have the listening student circle the level of proficiency they would give the presenter. Make sure students write an explanation for the grade they gave each category, using the back of the rubric to jot down their comments and suggestions for improvement. Remind students that constructive criticism is not personal and should include both positive comments and comments that suggest in a friendly manner an area needing improvement.

Once students have finished practising their presentations, allow them time to make revisions before their final presentations are due.

Grade students' presentations using the Rubric: Oral Presentation (2.1).

SURVIVING THE CITY TEACHER GUIDE © 2019 PORTAGE & MAIN PRESS ISBN: 978-1-55379-904-7

Date: _____   Name: _____

ORAL PRESENTATION

CATEGORY	Excellent	Good	Developing/Needs Improvement
Knowledge and Understanding /20	The presenter displays an in-depth knowledge about cultural activity, its historical context, as well as significance.	The presenter displays a decent amount of knowledge about the cultural activity but may be missing information about historical context or significance.	The presenter displays a limited knowledge about the cultural activity and its historical context and significance.
Visual Appeal /5	The presentation is highly appealing to the audience. Pictures and other multimedia are utilized throughout.	The presentation is somewhat appealing to the audience.	The presentation is not appealing to the audience.
Grammar & Spelling Conventions) /5	Writer makes no errors in grammar or spelling that distract the reader from the content on the multimedia presentation	Writer makes 1–2 errors in grammar or spelling that distract the reader from the content on the multimedia presentation.	Writer makes 3–4 errors in grammar or spelling that distract the reader from the content on the multimedia presentation.
Presentation Skills /5	The presenter maintains eye contact and appropriate tone/voice throughout the presentation	The presenter maintains some eye contact and appropriate tone/voice throughout the presentation	The presenter does not make eye contact and/or does not have appropriate tone/voice throughout the presentation

Total out of 35 marks: _____

WHAT IS WELLNESS FROM AN INDIGENOUS PERSPECTIVE?

DURATION

One hour

OVERVIEW

Schools often don't explicitly teach students how to be *well*. Throughout this lesson, students will learn about Indigenous perspectives of wellness relating to all parts of the self: physical, mental, emotional, and spiritual. Students will set goals in each category to facilitate holism, balance, and wellness in their lives. Students will learn the value of self-care, and why it is especially important while learning about difficult topics, such as those presented in *Surviving the City*.

MATERIALS

- Activity Sheet: Medicine Wheel Goal Setting (3.1) (one copy for each student)
- whiteboard
- markers
- writing utensils
- scrap paper

SURVIVING THE CITY TEACHER GUIDE © 2019 PORTAGE & MAIN PRESS ISBN: 978-1-55379-904-7

ACTIVATE: SELF-CARE WHOLE-CLASS DISCUSSION

Inform the class that today's lesson will be centred on the concept of wellness. Wellness as defined from an Indigenous perspective is when all the parts of ourselves—physical, spiritual, mental, and emotional—are in balance.

Begin the discussion by asking:
- What does it mean to be "well"?

Write students' answers on the whiteboard, so students have a visual as to what wellness might look and feel like. Inform students that wellness looks and feels different to different people, and that it is important for us to know what wellness looks and feels like for us personally.

ACQUIRE: MEDICINE WHEEL LESSON

For this part of the lesson, have students help you invite an Elder to speak to the class about the medicine wheel and its significance in Indigenous cultures. See "Inviting an Elder Into Your Learning Space" on page 4 for suggestions for inviting Elders to speak to students.

If this option is not available, there are many online resources that can help you explain the medicine wheel to your students, such as "The Seven Lessons of the Medicine Wheel" by Kelly J. Beaulieu.[25]

Hand out a copy of the Activity Sheet: Medicine Wheel Goal Setting (3.1) to each student. On the whiteboard, draw a large medicine wheel and label the four quadrants: "Physical," "Mental," "Spiritual," and "Emotional."

Explain that the four quadrants can represent many things, such as the four directions, the four phases of life, or the four sacred medicines.

Explain to students that they will use the medicine wheel to examine and think about the four parts of the self—physical, mental, spiritual, and emotional—and how it is important for the parts to be balanced if we truly want to be well. Advise students that we are also doing this activity to ensure that we can look after ourselves while learning about difficult topics, such as those presented in *Surviving the City*.

Provide students with information regarding the mental health supports that are available to them in the school and community. Teachers are encouraged to bring in a school counsellor to teach students about mental health and healthy coping skills. Create a list of healthy coping skills as a class, so students can choose the skills they are most likely to use to set goals.

SURVIVING THE CITY TEACHER GUIDE © 2019 PORTAGE & MAIN PRESS ISBN:978-1-55379-904-7

25 Beaulieu, Kelly J. "The Seven Lessons of the Medicine Wheel." *Say Magazine.* https://saymag.com/the-seven-lessons-of-the-medicine-wheel/

Have students set goals for themselves that fit each quadrant and write the goals on scrap paper. Explain that some goals may fit in two or more quadrants but to just pick the category that makes the most sense for them. It may be helpful to give some examples of goals for each quadrant:

- physical goals (health, fitness): I will lift weights once per week.
- spiritual goals (religious, focusing on self, family, community or anything that makes our "spirit" happy): I will practise my culture with my family once a month.
- mental goals (knowledge, school): I want to learn about outer space.
- emotional (mental health): I will practise deep breathing when I feel stressed.

Students should set at least three goals for each of the four quadrants.

APPLY: MEDICINE WHEEL GOAL SETTING ACTIVITY SHEET

Once students have at least three goals in each category, have them transform their goals into "SMART Goals." SMART stands for Specific, Measurable, Attainable, Realistic, and Time-bound. You may want to give students an example such as the following:

- Physical goal: I will eat healthy.

Notice how this goal is not in the SMART goal format, as it is not specific, measurable, nor time-bound. This goal should be changed to incorporate these elements:

- I will eat three servings of vegetables every day.
  OR
- I will limit myself to one sugary snack a day.

Have students fill in the Activity Sheet: Medicine Wheel Goal Setting (3.1) with their goals for the year using the SMART goal format. This really gets them thinking!

Finally, have students colour the four quadrants (physical = black, spiritual = yellow, mental = white, emotional = red).

ASSESS: MEDICINE WHEEL ASSESSMENT

Since this assignment is highly personal, it is often difficult to grade. An option is to have students read out three of their goals to you, so you can assess if the goals are SMART goals:

- Specific
- Measurable
- Achievable
- Realistic
- Time-bound

SURVIVING THE CITY TEACHER GUIDE © 2019 PORTAGE & MAIN PRESS ISBN: 978-1-55379-904-7

An example of a SMART goal is as follows:

· I will weight train once per week.

It is specific (instead of saying something vague like "I want to be stronger."); it is measurable, meaning you can easily identify if you accomplished the goal or not; it is achievable and realistic (you're not saying you are going to win a weight-lifting competition anytime soon, unless you are close to doing that already!); and it is time-bound, meaning you will do this every day, week, month, or year.

Alternatively, you can have students self-assess their progress in achieving their goals periodically throughout the year. This could involve asking students which goals they have been working on and which ones they need to improve on by either having a conversation with them or having them rate themselves on a scale of 1–10 and writing a small reflection on their progress, including successes and areas they still need to work on.

EXTENSION: CHECK-IN ACTIVITY

Throughout the year, you can also use the medicine wheel as a tool to check in on students' wellness.

Model how to do the check-in with your students. On the whiteboard, draw a large medicine wheel. Label the quadrants with the four parts of the self: Physical, Mental, Spiritual, and Emotional.

Explain to students that you are going to rate your own feelings of wellness today using the four categories. Draw a dot where you feel your own level of wellness is at today. Dots near the centre of the circle indicate you are not doing too well in that category, whereas dots near the outer edge of the circle indicate you feel well in that category. Connect your dots to form a circle shape. Circles that look like the medicine wheel indicate you are feeling well and balanced in all areas, whereas circles that look out of balance indicate you need to work on some areas today. See the following illustration as an example.

· **How I'm feeling today**

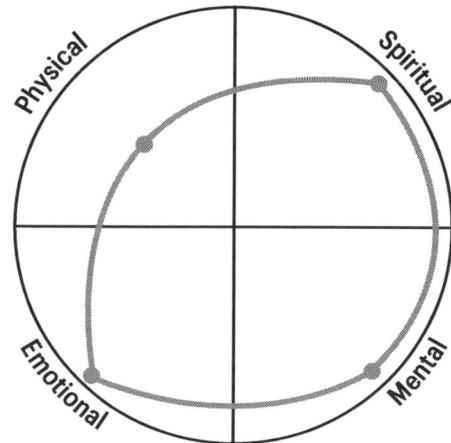

Meet one-on-one with each student to discuss their wellness levels, and have a conversation about how they can increase their wellness in areas that they rate lower. For example, if a student giving their physical wellness a low rating, have a discussion about why that is and what they can do to improve their wellness for tomorrow. For example, if a student often feels tired, they may want to work on going to bed earlier.

SURVIVING THE CITY TEACHER GUIDE © 2019 PORTAGE & MAIN PRESS   ISBN: 978-1-55379-904-7

Date: _____   Name: _____

MEDICINE WHEEL GOAL SETTING

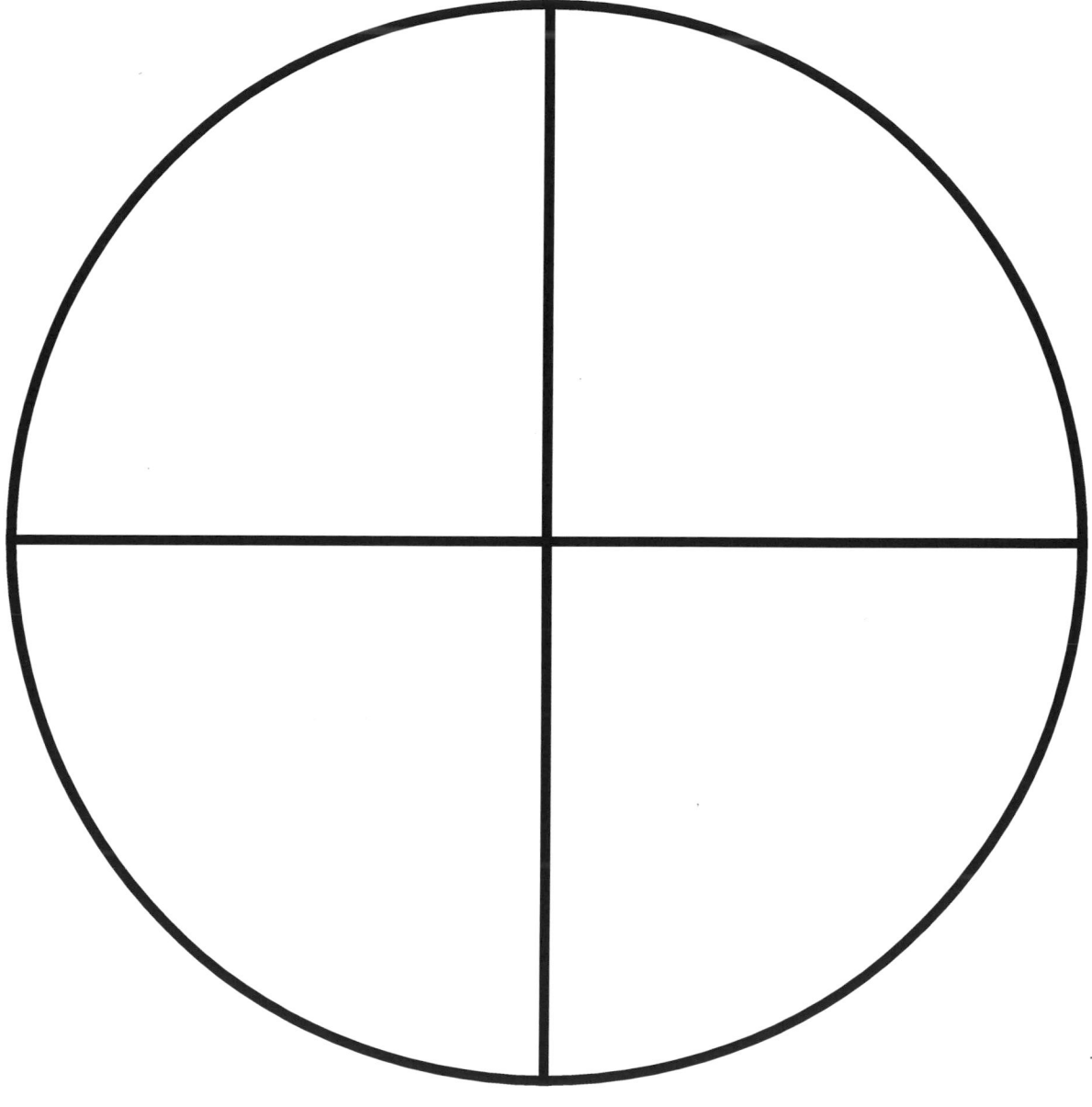

SURVIVING THE CITY TEACHER GUIDE © 2019 PORTAGE & MAIN PRESS   ISBN: 978-1-55379-904-7

3.1

LESSON 4

HOW CAN I MAKE A DIFFERENCE?

DURATION

Up to ten hours

Brainstorming: one hour

Lesson: one hour

Introduce project: one hour

Planning time: two hours

Preparation time: two hours

Implementation: one hour

Attending two other initiatives: two hours

OVERVIEW

Through this project, students will explore resistance in relation to the resurgence of Indigenous identity, culture, language, and land rights. First, students will explore worldwide resistance movements generally, and then focus in on the issue of Missing and Murdered Indigenous Women and Girls and Two-Spirit People as an issue that is deserving of attention and action. Students will have the opportunity to identify a social cause in their school, classroom, or community that they would like to tackle. They will be responsible for planning and implementing a social-justice action project, as well as attending and reflecting on other groups' action projects. The goal is that students will contribute to thoughtful, cooperative, and responsible social action, leading to active citizenship and engagement within their communities. This lesson and project can take anywhere from one to two months to complete, depending on the amount of class time students have to work on it.

SURVIVING THE CITY TEACHER GUIDE © 2019 PORTAGE & MAIN PRESS ISBN: 978-1-55379-904-7

MATERIALS
- chart paper
- markers
- computers/tablets with internet access
- Booklet: Social-Justice Action Project (4.1) (one copy for each student)
- Action Project Score Guide (4.2) (one copy for each student)

ACTIVATE: BRAINSTORM WORLDWIDE SOCIAL-JUSTICE ACTION INITIATIVES

Begin by posing the following questions to students, and soliciting responses:
- What is social justice? (the action of creating fairness for all people; rooted in human rights and equality)
- Why is social justice work important? (it gets people involved in thinking about solutions to problems in their communities and brings communities together in a positive way)
- What is social action? (taking steps to change the things that are wrong in our society and introducing new ideas and processes for doing things better in the future)
- Is there an example of social justice action in *Surviving the City*? What is it? (the Missing and Murdered Indigenous Women and Girls and Two-Spirit People march)

ACQUIRE: INDIGENOUS RESISTANCE LESSON

Put students into groups of three or four. Explain that they are going to conduct research and present to the class on an Indigenous Resistance Movement of their choice. Co-construct criteria for this short presentation with the class, such as:
- two to three minutes in length
- must include the 5 W's (who, what, when, where, why)
- must include at least three pictures

Have each group select an Indigenous Resistance Movement from across the continent, country, or their local territories. Some examples might include the following:
- **Idle No More** http://www.idlenomore.ca/
- **Standing Rock** https://americanindian.si.edu/nk360/plains-treaties/dapl.cshtml
- **Bear Clan Patrol** https://www.bearclanpatrolinc.com
- **Missing and Murdered Indigenous Women and Girls and Two-Spirit People**
  https://www.rcaanc-cirnac.gc.ca/eng/1448633299414/1534526479029
  https://www.cbc.ca/news/politics/mmiwg-inquiry-deliver-final-report-justice-re-forms-1.5158223
- **Barriere Lake Solidarity** http://www.barrierelakesolidarity.org
- **Klabona Keepers** https://warriorpublications.wordpress.com/tag/klabona-keepers/
- **Oshkimaadziig Unity Camp** https://ammsa.com/publications/windspeaker/camp-used-reconnect-people-traditional-agreements
- **Unist'ot'en Camp** https://unistoten.camp
- **The Yinka Dene Alliance** https://ammsa.com/publications/windspeaker/yinka-dene-alliance-group-british-columbia-first-nations

SURVIVING THE CITY TEACHER GUIDE © 2019 PORTAGE & MAIN PRESS ISBN: 978-1-55379-904-7

APPLY: IDEA JAM CAROUSEL ACTIVITY

Divide students into four groups. In their groups, have students read the recommendations in the report from the National Inquiry into Missing and Murdered Indigenous Women and Girls[26] and discuss ideas for their upcoming social-justice action projects.

Distribute a piece of chart paper and markers to each group. Assign each group a different type of social-justice action project to brainstorm around. The following are some examples of ideas they might discuss:

1) Educate/Raise Awareness
   - conduct research
   - prepare and deliver a class speech about an important issue
   - create a social media campaign
   - hand out pamphlets to educate others about an issue

2) Advocate for Change
   - write a letter to a Member of Parliament or to the school principal
   - arrange a meeting to discuss an issue with a local politician
   - start a school-wide petition

3) Support
   - fundraise for a local charity
   - attend and help out at a community event
   - volunteer at a local organization

4) Lead/Inspire/Change
   - start a school lunch group dedicated to your issue
   - create a social media campaign
   - create a friendship bench at your school

Give groups five minutes to discuss and write down all the possible ideas for their social-justice action projects they can think of in that category before they switch to the next station. As groups go from one station to the next, they are challenged to come up with new ideas that haven't been written down yet.

---

26 National Inquiry into Missing and Murdered Indigenous Women and Girls. "Reclaiming Power and Place: The Final Report of the National Inquiry into Missing and Murdered Indigenous Women and Girls." 2019. https://www.mmiwg-ffada.ca/final-report/

Once students have had a chance to brainstorm at each station, have them review the possibilities for their own social justice action projects.

Assign students a grade out of five based on their engagement in the group brainstorming activity.

APPLY: PLANNING YOUR ACTION PROJECT

Hand out a copy of the Booklet: Social-Justice Action Project (4.1) to each student. Explain that they will be working in groups of three to four to identify an issue they are passionate about, create a plan to address the issue in their classroom, school, or larger community, and then implement the plan.

Review the booklet with students, as well as the due dates for each section. Have students plan and implement their own social-justice action project in their group. Ensure students have adequate class time to plan and implement their project, and meet with students regularly to ensure that their projects are on track and feasible. Once students have their project date, time, and location planned, create a sign-up sheet for students to sign up to attend at least two other action projects.

APPLY: IMPLEMENTING YOUR ACTION PROJECT

Meet with each group periodically throughout the process to ensure that groups' plans are realistic and respectful. Make sure to attend all of the social-justice action project initiatives in order to effectively grade the assignment.

ASSESS: ACTION PROJECT SCORE GUIDE

Use the Action Project Score Guide (4.2) to assess students' research and reflections throughout the project.

SOCIAL-JUSTICE ACTION PROJECT

WHAT IS A SOCIAL-JUSTICE ACTION PROJECT?

An action project involves students working cooperatively to address a problem they see in their class, school or wider community. You will be working in groups of two or three to identify a social cause or problem, plan a community action project, and implement the project in your classroom, school, or wider community.

WHAT IS THE GOAL OF IMPLEMENTING A SOCIAL-JUSTICE ACTION PROJECT?

Students will contribute to thoughtful, cooperative, and responsible social action, leading to active citizenship and engagement with their communities.

PROJECT OVERVIEW

Step 1: Whole Class Brainstorm Idea Jam (5%)

What is your group's mission? How can you accomplish your mission?

Mission Examples
- Raise awareness about hunger in your city/town
- Create a safe space for 2SLGBTQ++ students
- Combat cyber bullying by creating a positive social media campaign

Step 2: Plan (30%)

Choose a mission and the best way your group can accomplish its mission and develop a proposal.

Step 3: Implement (50%)

Implement the plan! Actually create something or do something that positively affects the school and/or community and brings people together.

Step 4: Reflect (5 %)

Did your project work? What made it successful? What could have been done differently?

Step 5: Attend and Reflect on Other Initiatives (10%?)

Did you attend and reflect on at least two other initiatives?

SURVIVING THE CITY TEACHER GUIDE © 2019 PORTAGE & MAIN PRESS   ISBN: 978-1-55379-904-7

STEP 2: PLAN

Choose an issue and develop a plan to address/solve the issue.

ISSUE:_____

_____

_____

Explain the significance of your issue. Why does this issue matter? Who/what is affected by the issue? Why did you choose this particular issue?

_____

_____

_____

_____

_____

_____

_____

_____

_____

_____

_____

_____

_____

_____

_____

_____

_____

_____

SURVIVING THE CITY TEACHER GUIDE © 2019 PORTAGE & MAIN PRESS ISBN: 978-1-55379-904-7

4.1

_____

_____

_____

_____

_____

_____

_____

_____

_____

_____

_____

_____

Organizations that are already addressing this issue (List them in bullet form):

_____

_____

_____

_____

_____

_____

_____

_____

SURVIVING THE CITY TEACHER GUIDE © 2019 PORTAGE & MAIN PRESS   ISBN: 978-1-55379-904-7

What is your solution to your issue/problem? What are your action project goals/objectives?

_____

_____

_____

_____

_____

_____

_____

_____

_____

_____

_____

How are you going to ensure that people hear about your initiative? How will you ensure your plan will succeed?

_____

_____

_____

_____

_____

_____

_____

SURVIVING THE CITY TEACHER GUIDE © 2019 PORTAGE & MAIN PRESS   ISBN: 978-1-55379-904-7

4.1

Resources/Supplies Needed (List in bullet form):

_____

_____

_____

_____

_____

_____

_____

Who will do what? Assign roles.

_____

_____

_____

_____

_____

_____

_____

_____

_____

_____

_____

_____

SURVIVING THE CITY TEACHER GUIDE © 2019 PORTAGE & MAIN PRESS ISBN: 978-1-55379-904-7

4.1

Possible Problems and Concerns (as well as how they will be addressed):

_____

_____

_____

_____

_____

_____

_____

_____

_____

Timeline:

_____

_____

_____

_____

_____

_____

_____

_____

_____

_____

STEP 4: REFLECT

Did your project work? What made it successful? What could have been done differently?

SURVIVING THE CITY TEACHER GUIDE © 2019 PORTAGE & MAIN PRESS ISBN: 978-1-55379-904-7

STEP 5: ATTEND AND REFLECT ON OTHER INITIATIVES

Action Project Attended:

Date:

Response:_____

_____

_____

_____

_____

_____

_____

_____

Action Project Attended:

Date:

Response:_____

_____

_____

_____

_____

_____

_____

_____

SURVIVING THE CITY TEACHER GUIDE © 2019 PORTAGE & MAIN PRESS ISBN: 978-1-55379-904-7

4.1

ACTION PROJECT SCORE GUIDE

1. **BRAINSTORM 5%**
   i. Educate/Raise Awareness
   ii. Advocate for Change
   iii. Support
   iv. Lead/Inspire/Change

2. **PLAN 30%**
   i. Describe the significance of your issue.
   ii. Why does this issue matter?
   iii. Who/what is affected by the issue?
   iv. Why did you choose this particular issue?
   v. Organizations that are already addressing this issue:
   vi. What is your solution to your issue/problem?
   What are your action project goals/objectives?
   vii. How are you going to ensure that people hear about your initiative?
   How will you ensure your plan will succeed?
   viii. Assign Roles
   ix. Timeline
   x. Possible Problems and Concerns, as well as how they will be addressed.

3. **IMPLEMENTATION 50%   (TEACHER NOTES)**
   i. Did you attend and participate fully in your own implementation event?
   ii. Did you ensure the event was successful?
   iii. Did you attend to any issues that may have arose?
   iv. Did you leave a lasting impression on people?

4. **REFLECT 5%**
   i. How did your event go?
   ii. What would you do differently next time?

5. **ATTEND AND REFLECT ON OTHER INITIATIVES 10%**
   i. Did you attend at least two other initiatives and reflect thoughtfully on them?

SURVIVING THE CITY TEACHER GUIDE © 2019 PORTAGE & MAIN PRESS   ISBN: 978-1-55379-904-7

4.2

ISBN:978-1-55379-904-7

*Thank you to Tasha Spillett for creating a beautiful work of literature
in which students can see reflections of themselves, their families, and their communities.*
—CM

Design by Jennifer Lum
22 21 20 19   1 2 3 4 5

PORTAGE &
MAIN PRESS

www.portageandmainpress.com
Winnipeg, Manitoba
Treaty 1 Territory and homeland of the Métis Nation